The Robots' Rebellion

The story of the Spiritual Renaissance

DAVID ICKE

Gateway Books, Bath

Published in 1994 by
GATEWAY BOOKS
The Hollies, Wellow,
Bath, BA2 8QJ, U.K.

First printing July 1994
Fifth printing, December 1997
Copyright © 1994 by David Icke

Distributed in the U.S.A. by
Access Publishers
6893 Sullivan Road
Grawn, MI 49637

Cover designed by Nick Gonzales
printed by Potten, Baber & Murray
Text set in 10¹/₂ on 12¹/₂ by
Oak Press of Castleton
Printed and bound by
Redwood Books of Trowbridge

British Library Cataloguing-in Publication Data:
A catalogue record for this book is
available from the British Library

ISBN 1-85860-022-7

Contents

Dedication

To Thomas Paine, Socrates, Arthur Findlay, Sir George Trevelyan, and all who have, through courage and love, sought to challenge the suppression of knowledge and the indoctrination of the human race.
To Alick and all at Gateway for having the courage to publish this book.

Introduction

What is the big question we need to answer?

A scientist talking on television recently said the Big Question was 'How was the Universe formed?' But is it?

Is that really the answer we must find above all others at a time of such trauma and confusion on this planet? I would say not. I think that how the Universe was formed is extremely interesting, but not something that it is essential to know in order to find the path that will lead us out of this mess.

What we really need to know – the Big Question – is who we really are and what we are doing here in this period of fantastic change and transformation on Planet Earth. From that understanding, all the other answers will come – including how the Universe was formed. Without that appreciation of the true nature of life, we will go on being mesmerised by this physical world and largely controlled by its illusions and by those misguided forces, detailed in this book, which seek to turn us into little more than zombies. In other words, we will destroy ourselves.

The irony is that the information already exists to tell us all we need to know, but the implications of this knowledge are so catastrophic for religion, establishment science, education (indoctrination) and the whole economic, political, industrial, and military system, that these answers have been suppressed. When suppression has not been possible, those who articulate the eternal understanding have been ridiculed, condemned and undermined in every way imaginable. We still refer to the Great Mysteries of Life, but they only remain 'mysteries' because of the consequences for the system of their solution. We are talking here of the most monumental con-trick in the history of the human race, a sleight of hand and mind that involves not only people, but other areas of the Universe too. It has been a piece of black magic so successful that it has programmed the minds of billions of people to forget who they are, where they came from, and what they are doing here today.

I believe it is time for some straight talking. We are a race of robots. By that, I mean that most people do not have a thought in their heads that has not been put there by someone or something else. We have become a race of programmed minds which can be persuaded to believe and do almost anything as long as the drip, drip, drip of lies and misinformation continues to bombard us through our political systems, the media, religion, schools, universities, and by infiltration of our consciousness by other universal sources which want to turn Planet Earth into a zombies' prison. But, slowly at first and now ever more quickly, the robots are awakening. Instead of meekly accepting a daily diet of mind control, more and more people are seeing the world in a new light and asking questions they have never asked before. The veil is lifting and the robots' rebellion has arrived.

In this book, I will tell the story of how we forgot our true identity and how the forces of control are preparing to enter the final phase of their plan to take over the planet and the human race. Humanity has been gripped by a spiritual amnesia which has taken us down a dark and dangerous path from which we are now in the process of escaping, or not, depending on the choices we make. Most of what you are about to read will not be new to you. You already know it. You have merely forgotten. You have a memory that retains some of what you have experienced in this physical lifetime, but humanity has lost contact with its higher memory; that part of us which knows the Big Answers to the Big Questions. This book will help you to restore the links with that memory and, once that begins to happen, as it has already begun for countless millions around the world today, you are never going to be the same again.

Those who are moving along this road to rediscovery are the ones who are leading the robots' rebellion. It is vital for the future of the human race for as many as possible to wake up and set out on that same journey. Only by triggering and expanding a reconnection with our higher levels of being will we have access to the information and love that we so desperately need in order to heal ourselves and, through that, to help to heal this beautiful planet we call Earth. We stand on the threshold of indescribable and incomprehensible change. We cannot know exactly what will unfold, because humans are affecting the detail with every passing minute, but we can be sure that nothing and no-one will be left untouched by what is happening on the planet. I believe these changes are the harbingers of a far, far, better world than the one we survey today. I think it was Voltaire who said: "Those who believe absurdities commit atrocities". Humanity over many centuries is the living proof of that.

We are in the time of awakening when believing absurdities will be part of human history and no longer the very foundations of human life.

David Icke,
Ryde, Isle of Wight, June 1994

A Definition of Wisdom

How can you buy or sell the sky? We do not own the freshness of the air or the sparkle on the water. How then can you buy them from us? Every part of the Earth is sacred to my people, holy in their memory and experience. We know the white man does not understand our ways. He's a stranger who comes in the night and takes from the land whatever he needs. The Earth is not his friend but his enemy, and when he's conquered it he moves on. He kidnaps the Earth from his children. His appetite will devour the Earth and leave behind a desert. If the beasts were gone we would die from a great loneliness of the spirit, for whatever befalls the Earth, befalls the children of the Earth.

Chief Seattle, 1854

Remember Who You Are

A theme thoughout this book is the story of a conspiracy to control the human race. That may sound fantastic to you at this stage, but read on and you will see that it is very real and affecting our lives every day. It is, however, a conspiracy that we can, and will, dismantle.

At the heart of this attack on human freedom is the desire to keep from us the knowledge of the spiritual realities of our true selves and the understanding of our place in this wondrous web of life we call Creation. *If you have heard the explanations about the eternal nature of consciousness and how we are all on an endless journey of evolution through experience, it is fine to move straight on to the first chapter.* If such information is new to you it is worth reading the following short summary of the knowledge. The manipulators know this information is correct, but they don't want you to know that:

The real us is not the physical body we see. That is the vehicle we inhabit for a single physical lifetime on this planet. The eternal us is our consciousness, our spirit, our mind. At that moment we mistakenly call 'death' our eternal mind – the thinking, feeling, us – leaves the body and moves on to continue its evolution elsewhere.

This is what happens in a so-called 'near death experience'. Thousands have described the sensation of leaving their bodies during heart attacks or road accidents. They tell the same basic story of looking down on their physical bodies while doctors try to revive them. "It was my mind, my personality, looking down", they say, "but I was no longer part of my body." Then suddenly they find themselves looking out through their eyes again and they have returned to the body. This is all that happens to people when they 'die'. Their consciousness leaves the body. Our physical form has a finite life, of course, but our minds live forever. You could think of it as similar to the principle of the spaceman on the Moon. He dons an outer shell to experience another planet. During a physical life our minds inhabit the physical shell we call a body.

Consciousness and energy are one and the same. All that exists throughout Creation is the same energy-consciousness in different states of being. The difference between everything is their level of consciousness (evolution, understanding, awareness), and the speed the energy is vibrating – its 'frequency'. The faster the vibration, the higher the evolution. One example of how a single substance can be many things is water, clouds and ice. These look, feel, and react very differently, but they are all the same substance in different states of being. So it is with the energy-consciousness that is everything.

The force we call 'God' is not some guy with a beard sitting on a throne. It is the One Consciousness that is Creation; a wall, the sky, the rain, you, me, everything is 'God'. We are all droplets in the same ocean of consciousness. You are me, and I am you. You are everything, and so am I. We are each other, all aspects of the same whole, part of the same seamless stream of energy. The apparent divisions between us are an illusion.

One of the so-called 'great mysteries' is where we go after our physical lives have ended. The Church says to heaven or hell, whatever that is supposed to mean, and materialistic science says we go nowhere because this world is all there is. In fact the ocean of consciousness we call Creation or God has infinite levels of evolution or wavelengths. In the space your body is occupying now are all the frequencies of all the radio and television stations broadcasting to your area. You can't see them and they can't see each other, even though they are sharing the same space, because they are on different wavelengths. Tune a radio to one of those wavelengths and that is the station you will hear. The frequency becomes the radio's reality, its 'world'. Move the dial to another station and the radio's reality changes. It is the same with us. At this time we are tuned to the dense physical wavelength we call the Universe, but when we 'die' our consciousness leaves the body and moves on to another wavelength.

What we call 'ghosts' are entities – minds, spirits, – on other wavelengths. They often look misty and transparent because we are not seeing them from their frequency, but ours. It is the same when a radio dial is not quite on the station and you get a fuzzy, less-than-sharp reception. The dominating station will be the one nearest the dial but you will hear other stations, too. In visual terms, that is what is happening when we see a ghost. If you were on the same frequency as the ghost, it would look as real as you do.

The extra-terrestrials I will be talking about operate mostly on other frequencies, which is why some people see them and some don't. It depends whether you are capable of making that psychic leap to tune to other levels.

It is by tuning your consciousness to another wavelength that information can be brought through to this world. This is the process we call channelling, mediumship, or tuning in psychically. Real, open-minded scientists are showing in their research into physics and mathematics that Creation is, indeed, made up of frequencies, and that consciousness is eternal in everyone. However, they have to contend with the suppression of this knowledge by the scientific establishment and the manipulators who control it. These want you to believe that the physical world is all there is and that we are all cosmic 'accidents' of evolution who don't exist before birth or after death. What nonsense!

Consciousness is constantly reproducing itself as Creation expands into the void and into infinity. At the highest level, the highest frequency, is the original consciousness from which everything has come. It is the sum total of all that has been learned and experienced since Creation became conscious. This is the level you could call the Godhead. I prefer to call it the Source. It, too, is constantly evolving by observing and absorbing the experiences of all aspects of itself on the lower frequencies. The Source is the Super Mind from which everything has come.

I have used the term 'mind' to describe the eternal part of us, because I prefer to avoid the religious connotations of 'soul'. But mind, soul, and spirit are interchangeable terms to describe the amalgamation of energy fields that animate the physical body and which never die. These exist on what science calls the sub-atomic level which is why we can't see them. The energies normally vibrate too quickly for our physical senses, although some sensitive people can detect them. When we talk of people 'seeing auras' they are observing this consciousness around the body. It can be a glorious tapestry of colours, our 'coat of many colours' which changes with our moods because colours, like everything else, are energy vibrations. As our state of mind alters, so do the subtleties of our vibrational state.

These energy fields, aspects of our mind, reincarnate into countless physical bodies on this planet and elsewhere. We are all extra-terrestrials, in that we are here on this planet as part, and only part, of our evolution. Each of us will have had past lives throughout what we call history. We have been here many times in so many different situations and races. This makes the prejudice of racism and nationalism so utterly ludicrous. Through the law of karma or cause and effect we are creating our own futures with every thought and act, because it is true that what we make others experience we will ourselves eventually experience to balance out our evolution.

Connecting all our energy fields is a series of vortices called chakras. There are seven main ones and countless smaller versions. The main chakras are at the base of the spine (base chakra), the navel (sacral chakra), the solar plexus (solar plexus chakra), the heart (heart chakra), the throat (throat chakra), the forehead (brow or third eye chakra) and on top of the head (crown chakra). As we learn and evolve, the chakra vortices spin quicker and raise the vibration of our eternal being, so elevating us to higher frequencies. The energy we call love comes from the heart chakra and this is how the heart first became associated with love. Today it is portrayed as a physical heart, but, as the ancients knew, the energy of love emanates from the spiritual heart.

The chakras are linked to the physical body through the endocrine system, and imbalances in the energy fields can affect the balance of the body. It is in this way that stress and other emotional trauma cause physical illness. These energy fields are electromagnetic and are affected by other forms of electromagnetism. It is known that people who work with electromagnetic equipment or live under power lines are more prone to certain illnesses and cancers. Doctors and scientists say they don't know why this happens, but in fact the electromagnetism from the power lines and technology disrupts the person's electromagnetic energy fields, and this filters down to the physical body to manifest as a health problem.

The mind is a creator because everything is thought. The more powerful the consciousness, the greater its potential to create. On the non-physical frequencies thought creates directly by rearranging the energies into whatever the thought visualises. Even on the dense physical level, all creation must be preceded by a thought. A finalised business deal and a finished piece of pottery are thoughts made physical. Thought is all.

Every time we think we create an energy field, a thought form, and this is how telepathy works. One person produces the thought field and another decodes that field, mostly without even knowing it. The power of thought to create love and harmony or hate and disharmony is endless and we are all capable of producing both. The manipulators I speak of in this book know about this power to control people by the use of thought or 'psychic attack' as it is called. They direct thought energy at targeted individuals and try to control their thinking. Those who seek love and harmony in the world need to respond to this misguided behaviour with the energy of love and harmony which we can all create whenever we wish. We just have to think it and live it. We create our own reality. If we think failure, that is the energy we will attract to us. We attract what we most fear, for example, on the principle of like attracts like and this is the basis on which the Law of Karma operates also.

The manipulators do not want us to know that we are eternal beings of light and love with limitless potential; nor that we can change the world by changing the way we think; and certainly not that we are all One, all equal parts of the same whole, on a journey of evolution through experience. People who know and live all these things are not nearly so easy to control and direct. It would be much better to persuade us that we are cosmic accidents with no future, or imprison us in the dogma of some rigid religion, and do everything possible to ridicule and repress information to the contrary.

Their aim is to de-link us from the higher levels of ourselves. During an incarnation, not all of our mind, consciousness, incarnates and becomes subject to the severe pressures and limitations of a dense physical body, only part of it. I call this the conscious level. The rest of the mind, what has become known as the subconscious and higher conscious levels, act as a guide through a physical life. The conscious level (lower self) experiences and the subconscious and higher conscious levels (higher self) guides through a process of thought transfer.

The higher self can be likened to Mission Control. It knows the reason for the incarnation – what we have chosen to experience and who with – and what we have chosen to do in service to humanity, the planet, and Creation in general. We feel the urgings and communciations of the higher self in our intuition. We feel drawn to certain places, people, and ways of life. It shows when we say "fancy meeting you here", "what a small world", and "what a coincidence".

If we lose touch with Mission Control, our higher consciousness, we can get ourselves into terrible trouble and be prone to some stupid and destructive behaviour. Think what would happen if we were on the Moon in a spacesuit and someone cut the link with Mission Control. We would have only two sources of information – what is coming in through the eyes and the ears. This would, by definition, be extremely imbalanced, because it would only contain information from the world immediately around us. We would lose contact with those who can see the wider picture.

So if we can be encouraged to switch off the connection with our personal Mission Control, the higher self, and the manipulators can at the same time control the flow of information coming in through the eyes and the ears, we can quite easily forget who we really are and what we are doing here. This has happened to billions of people, who have thus become a form of robot.

I have explained these principles in greater depth in other books, and it would be helpful for those new to the subject to read *Heal The World* or *Truth Vibrations* in conjunction with this one. But within the brief summary here is contained the knowledge as you will appreciate later that can not only free the human race from its current mental imprisonment, but also provide incredible technology to produce limitless, non-polluting energy.

Why and how this knowledge has been kept from the mass of the people and what has led humanity along such a dark and destructive path is the story we will now tell.

PART ONE

THE DARKNESS

1

The Takeover Bid

WHEN anyone talks about the origin of God they soon find themselves facing familiar, unanswerable questions: 'Who created God?' and 'Who created the one who created God?' and...

You will forgive me, therefore, if I deal with only one generation of God's family history! My belief is that what we call Creation was once a void that was mere potential. At some point, at least a part of this void became conscious and aware of itself. I know some open-minded scientists who have offered explanations based on mathematics and physics of how this could have happened, but all I am sure about is that it did happen.

I will call this original consciousness The Source. Over an incomprehensible period of what we call time the Source consciousness began to experiment with its potential to create. Through the power of thought, it created other aspects of itself and areas within its vast mind for experience and learning. Among these was our Universe and all that it contains – including us. Each area is relatively self-contained within the Ocean of Consciousness and has been allowed to evolve naturally through experience, although all remains connected to the Source. Universes, like all of Creation, are made up of multi-dimensions with each having its own version of space and time. What we call time on this planet is very different from that of other frequencies. If you saw our space-time Universe from above, it would look a little like a doughnut or, more to the point, a coil going round and round, orbiting the centre. Everything is in orbit around a central point. The Earth is orbiting the Sun, as we all know, but the solar system is also in orbit, as are the galaxy and the Universe. Each 'coil' is encircled within a vortex, a spiral of energy. The quicker this spiral vortex spins, the quicker the Universe moves through its orbit and, consequently, the quicker 'time' appears to pass. The vortex around our Universe is beginning to spin more quickly which is

2

why when so many people say, 'time just flies these days, there's no time to do everything any more', they are absolutely right. Hold on tight. We have seen nothing yet.

Streams of information emanate from The Source to guide Creation while, from the other direction, flow all the experiences and learning achieved by its constituent parts. There is a two-way flow of information between the Source and all areas of its mind. So, while the Source is the ultimate in knowledge, wisdom and love at any given point, it, too, is constantly evolving as it absorbs the experiences of all its 'droplets'. The flow of information from the Source comes to this planet via various 'sub-stations' such as the Universe and Galaxy. It comes in through the Sun to the planets of this solar system. Each level adds its contribution to the information flow to guide the levels below. The Sun is far more than a massive ball of fire, generating warmth. It is another sub-station for Source energies. The ancients knew this, or at least their most highly-evolved members did, and this is one explanation for the origin of the Sun god and Sun worship. The more enlightened members of their number were not worshipping a ball of fire in the sky, they were acknowledging the Solar Logos (Central Sun) through which the knowledge and wisdom of the Source reaches the planet.

Just as the Sun is the mind that guides the solar system, the Galactic Mind guides the galaxy and the Universal Mind guides the Universe. The Source is the mind that guides all Creation. Sun spot activity is linked to this flow of energy from the Sun to the solar system and this indicates the times when the flow is at its most powerful. We all have the opportunity to tune into this guidance from the highest level, the Source, but we don't have to. We can ignore it if we wish.

It may seem hard to believe sometimes when we look at what is happening in the world, but Creation is another word for love. It is the energy we call love that holds everything together. Creation is not designed to bring pain and suffering. That is not its purpose. I know that people from all beliefs and backgrounds have tried to explain this contradiction between a Creation based on love and some of the appalling events that happen minute by minute on Planet Earth. Some speak of the need for learning through extreme experience while others talk of some massive universal 'experiment' that has been going on. Neither has felt right to me. If Creation is founded and held together by love, then love must be at the heart of what has happened to the Earth and the human race. Just as this book was being completed, I heard an explanation which made more sense to me. I was sitting in the quiet of the abbey ruins on a wonderful summer day at Glastonbury in Somerset, England, not far from the famous Glastonbury Tor. With me was a very close friend of my family and myself, a highly sensitive psychic called Yeva. She began to channel information projected by a blue energy field she saw psychically around us. From what came through that day and from the other information I have received directly or through other channels, I feel that the following is close to the truth, at least in theme, symbolically, not literally.

A very long time ago, an aspect of consciousness became highly imbalanced and decided to challenge the laws of Creation. These were not laws written down in a book and administered by a judge. They were, you might say, like the laws of physics. Everything needs a negative-positive and male-female balance if harmony is to reign in its consciousness. The balance does not have to be perfect, because both negative and positive experiences are necessary for evolution. But the further you stray from balance, the more extreme life becomes. If you go too far to the positive polarity you lose touch with the practical side of life; you float off in a spiritual mist. It's a bit like the feeling I am told you have when you smoke pot or, as I can report from experience, the feeling you have after drinking a few beers. You are not quite here. Everyone can be very nice to everyone else, but nothing gets done. If you have a serious negative imbalance, this will manifest itself in extreme negative behaviour – anger, aggression, conflict, a wish to control and dominate, pain, fear and suffering in all its forms.

I will call the droplet seeking to disharmonise Creation, Lucifer. I will use the term Lucifer when I am speaking of the original droplet of disharmony and Luciferic consciousness when I am describing the amalgamation of that aspect and all the other consciousness he has since imbalanced, to the extent that it now dances to his tune. In fact, Lucifer is a misnomer really, in that, if you go back to the origin of the name Lucifer, it breaks down as 'bringer of light'. This comes from the universal truth that positive energy needs a negative balancer. When both are in harmony, you get the energy of balance and love which is called The Light. The positive needs the negative as much as the negative needs the positive. This idea of the balancing of two forces, positive-negative, male-female, good–evil, yin–yang and so on, I totally agree with. But, for the purposes of this book, I will use the name Lucifer to describe something quite different from that. The imbalanced consciousness I will call Lucifer is not an essential part of the positive-negative balance. He is a disrupting, disharmonious aspect of consciousness which is not necessary for human evolution. More than that, Lucifer's efforts to close off the channels that link humanity to its higher understanding have blocked, not advanced, our evolution. No experience is wasted and all goes into the bank of learning, but I feel strongly that we did not need to plumb the depths in order to reach the state of understanding that will raise us to a higher frequency. A balance of negative and positive experience is one thing, but I do not believe the negative extremes we have seen on Earth have had to be part of that.

Lucifer wished to experiment with the laws of balance and harmony. I refer to this mind as 'he' because he is dominated, not only by negative energy, but by male energy also. At one time he was a consciousness of balance, love and advanced evolution – but that was to change. It may well be that something happened which was beyond his control but which initially imbalanced this aspect of consciousness. It could be that an experiment he conducted into what would happen if you opposed the laws of harmony went terribly wrong – rather like creating a spiritual Frankenstein which ends up controlling the scientist. Whatever the background, Lucifer began to challenge the harmony of Creation. I have long been aware of this but Yeva's channelling added a piece to the puzzle. It answered the question of why humanity has been a target of this Luciferic consciousness.

Creation is not some random, uncoordinated, every-droplet-for-itself chaos. When this Luciferic consciousness began to make its disharmony felt, the higher levels of Creation began to intervene because it was imposing its misunderstandings on others and breaking the universal law of free will. Something had to be done, as they say. This is where humanity comes in. Again, contrary to popular belief, the human consciousness stream has an enormous capacity for love and compassion. We are not what we seem to be, but then nothing is ever what it seems. A decision was made at the collective level of human consciousness to give this disruptive mind called Lucifer an opportunity to find its balance again and to re-synchronise with the rest of Creation.

Every species has a collective mind to which all of the individual 'droplets' are connected. We are multi-dimensional beings, with each level having its own awareness and ability to think and make decisions. So it was that the collective mind of humanity agreed to set aside its own evolution for a certain period to give the Luciferic consciousness a chance to re-balance itself. This highly negative consciousness was unleashed on this part of the Universe. It was not only humanity which agreed to this, the collective minds of other universal civilisations (extra-terrestrials) did the same, and not only the physical level was affected. Everything is multi-dimensional, including the Universe. In the same space occupied by this physical world are all the other levels. The Luciferic consciousness began to operate on those levels, too.

The effects did not happen overnight. But disharmony creates more disharmony and, once the Luciferic consciousness had begun to disrupt the balance and flow of the energies, it started a roll which would gather pace on an ever-steepening curve. Disharmony created even more disharmony. Lucifer is clearly not a being with horns and a tail. He is a large aspect of Divine consciousness which chose to work against the Source. Like all consciousness, he generates thought patterns. It is the same principle as that employed by a radio station when it transmits its wavelength to the world. Once transmitted, the wavelength can be picked up by any radio tuned to that station. Everyone is transmitting thought patterns every second. So, when you have a powerful and ever-growing aspect of consciousness pouring out negative patterns of great disharmony, it is easy to see how vast areas of other consciousness can be affected. Once they are tuned to your wavelength you can, like a radio station, feed them any information you wish them to hear. In consciousness terms, these transmitted patterns can appear to be thoughts of our own when they really originate in the minds of others. In such instances, we are merely tuning to them without realising it.

The Luciferic consciousness and its broadcasts were designed to create imbalance. Lucifer feeds off negative energy and the more of that that he can generate, the stronger and more powerful he becomes. His impact began to grow and affect a wider area. Other droplets were imbalanced by the disharmony and turmoil and joined the 'team' or what I call collectively the Luciferic consciousness. The thinking and perceptions of increasing numbers of entities in this solar system and galaxy were affected. The Luciferic consciousness, far from taking the opportunity to re-balance itself, was trying to take over and turn harmony into the image of its own imbalance. The moment arrived when the ongoing process of disharmony was such that a call went out across the Universe for volunteers to dedicate themselves, for however long was necessary, to reverse it. The ocean of consciousness was ceasing to be a gentle, balanced flow. In some areas it was more like a tidal wave of emotional and mental turmoil and torment. Throughout the book I will refer to the 'volunteers' or 'volunteer consciousness'. By this I mean those who have dedicated themselves to restore harmony and help the Earth to re-synchronise with the rest of the Galactic and Universal family. These volunteers came forward on many levels and the struggle began between light and dark, a theme seen throughout ancient texts and legends. This has been portrayed symbolically in films like *Star Wars* and *The Empire Strikes Back*. The writers of much science fiction are really tapping into a memory of what actually happened, not always in detail, but in theme. This struggle between harmony and disharmony has been happening on all levels, physical and non-physical.

Other volunteers, aspects of very highly-evolved consciousness, came into the Universe and this galaxy in an effort to restore harmony. They did not incarnate in physical bodies on the Earth. They arrived in massive spacecraft, some of them miles in length, while others simply manifested themselves here. These were extra-terrestrials who came to bring knowledge to this planet hundreds of thousands of years ago. There were two distinct life streams on the planet then, the highly evolved extra-terrestrials and the much more primitive Earth people. The idea was that, over thousands of years, the Earth people would be helped to evolve more quickly.

Waves of these beings began many civilisations on the Earth, including the ones we know as Pan, Mu (Lemuria) and Atlantis. These civilisations were much more advanced in their technology and understanding of Creation than we are today. Plato talked of Atlantis more than two thousand years ago and it has been a theme that has recently grown more powerful in the human mind. It was a continent in what is now the Atlantic Ocean. Atlantis was powered by the use of non-physical energy, the harnessing of the sea of energy around us. Crystals were part of this power and light source and all the power and warmth they needed was produced without any pollution or damage to the Earth. That knowledge is going to be available to us as the present transformation continues. Indeed, much of it is already available but has been suppressed to protect empires of self interest. There was no religion as such at that time but there were places where people went to learn the laws of Creation and how to use energies to create harmony and to speed the positive progress of human understanding. They could communicate with animals telepathically and through sound, particularly with that most evolved of non-human life, the dolphin. The Atlanteans could perform what we would see today as miracles. They were not miracles at all. There is no such thing as a miracle or the paranormal. They are simply the natural laws of Creation at work. Atlanteans could levitate objects and themselves at will; they could cause spontaneous combustion; they could manifest and de-manifest matter. They raised its vibratory rate until it ceased to be physical. Then, when they restored its original vibration, it reappeared as a physical form.

Their bodies were different from ours and very different from those of the Earth people on the planet at that time. They were less dense and they could float above the ground through the power of their consciousness. Many could materialise and de-materialise themselves along the lines of 'Beam me up, Scotty' in *Star Trek* but without the need for its technology. They were much taller than we are. Sensitive people who have had visions of this Atlantean time speak of seeing figures of seven feet and more, with gold complexions and slanting, pale blue eyes. The Atlanteans also lived for many hundreds of years in each incarnation because their bodies were more in tune with the energies around them. As they understood the true nature of life, they could treat disease (disharmony) before it became a physical problem. Today we wait for the physical symptoms but, by then, it is often too late. The volunteer consciousness which are known as Lemurians and Atlanteans came to raise the understanding on this planet in order to help the Luciferic consciousness to break out of its spiral of disharmony and to protect the human consciousness from being affected by that disharmony.

All was well in Lemuria and Atlantis for a long time, but slowly the imbalances and pressures which continued to build up under the bombardment of the Luciferic consciousness began to tell. Over aeons of existence, the Luciferic consciousness had learned how best to disrupt harmony and how to imbalance other aspects by working through their emotional levels. The production of negative energy by whatever means available was the motivation because such negative energy feeds it and gives it greater power.

The reason for conflict was irrelevant as long as there was conflict and a production line of negative energy. Planets were destroyed, either by direct intervention from Lucifer or by his thought patterns scrambling the consciousness of others. A planet known by the Sumerians as Maldek was destroyed by nuclear explosion created by scientists who had the knowledge without the wisdom. (See Allan & Delair's *When The Earth Nearly Died*). Some of the debris of that planet and others is still flying around the solar system in forms we call asteroids and comets. Some of the debris is held in the rings of Saturn. Too incredible to accept? Look what we are doing to this planet. We are destroying her by the way in which we behave and that is what has happened elsewhere, either through exploitation, nuclear explosions, or by the poisoning of the atmosphere in some other way. Has humanity as a whole been under the influence of a force for good? No. Exactly.

The time arrived when Luciferic extra-terrestrials sought to take over the planet and wars were fought between the, by now, countless extra-terrestrial civilisations that wished to either help or exploit this world. The harmony of early Atlantis had long gone. The Earth which was created as the planet of balance and a generator of love began to pour out negative energy into the system. Things were going terribly wrong and it was having a serious affect on the mind of the planet, the consciousness we call Mother Nature, the Earth Spirit, or Gaia. The Earth is the dense physical body of this mind and we all exist within her energy field, her aura. When humanity creates negative energy she absorbs it and, through her, it is exported to the solar system, the Universe, and beyond. Lucifer turned his negative power on the Earth Spirit, working to disrupt her on all levels by imbalancing her energy fields – especially her mind and emotions. His thought patterns worked on her emotions both directly and by affecting her physical form. When our bodies are giving us pain it affects our emotions. A planet consciousness is no different. The extra-terrestrial volunteers who agreed to restore harmony and to raise consciousness on the physical level found themselves facing an enormous challenge from other extra-terrestrial sources who came to the planet in their enormous spacecraft. Many were so affected that they, also, began to work for the negative forces.

Knowledge is neutral. It is how you use it that is positive or negative. Those who understood the use of energies and the power of crystals were known in Atlantis and Lemuria as the Guardians of the Light and the Keepers of the Secret Knowledge. Only those who, it was felt, could be trusted to use the knowledge positively were told of its secrets. However, here we had a situation where the power of the Lucifer influence was such that many of these people had become seriously imbalanced. As a consequence, knowledge which was potentially lethal was falling into the wrong hands. Many Atlanteans began to use their knowledge in highly negative ways as did the extra-terrestrials who hijacked Atlantis.

For hundreds of thousands of years during Atlantis and earlier, extra-terrestrials from various universal civilisations had been seeding the human race and advancing the physical form. Some did this for positive reasons, some with their own agenda in mind. The themes of this are documented in ancient texts and on clay tablets written some 6,000 years ago by the Sumerians. The Sumer records speak of 'gods' coming down from the sky to impregnate women and then returning to the stars. The human form as we know it, *Homo Sapiens Sapiens* to give it its full title, did not evolve from the ape family but from other universal civilisations around 20,000 years or so before the final cataclysm sank what remained of Atlantis about 10,000BC. In fact, the ape family came from the impregnation of animal forms by ETs as part of their experimentation. Scientists talk of the 'missing link' between Neanderthal man and the present human body, but they will never find it, because it doesn't exist. The sudden evolutionary advance in the human form came from the intervention of extra-terrestrials, some positive in their intent, some negative.

The Sumer records say that a 'god' called Ea was involved in this genetic engineering. They say he had a half-brother called En-lil and, as we will see, these were two of the Sumer 'gods' that would be passed on into the belief systems of religions to this day. Most of the early Old Testament stories come from Sumer or earlier and relate to this time towards the end of Atlantis when negative ETs were largely in control. A Sumerian 'hymn' has been discovered which describes the tree of life, the fruit of which the gods had forbidden Man to eat. This tree was in the Garden of Edinnu, a word which means plain. In this garden, according to the hymn, you would find the god, Ea. How short a step this is to Adam and Eve and the Garden of Eden in the Bible. The Sumer depiction of the Garden of Edinnu even included a snake curled around a tree. The Garden of Edinnu and its recycled version, the Garden of Eden, are highly symbolic of what was happening from the later

Atlantis period and is still happening today. Adam and Eve (symbolising Earth Man and Woman) were told not to eat from the tree of knowledge. In other words, they were to be kept in ignorance so that they would not learn of their true nature. This is a theme which has continued throughout human history up to the present day. I call it 'the Mushroom Approach' – keep them in the dark and feed them bullshit.

According to William Bramley, in his book *The Gods of Eden*, the serpent in the Adam and Eve story is symbolic of something called the Brotherhood of the Snake (or serpent) which he believes was set up to give spiritual knowledge to an ignorant humanity by those who wished to help them. Bramley's research leads him to suggest that the 'god' known as Ea, or Prince of Earth, by the Sumerians who helped to create and genetically engineer the new human form, did not wish to see them mentally, spiritually, and physically imprisoned. He did some less-than-advisable things himself, Bramley believes, but he was genuine in his desire to challenge this oppression. Unfortunately, the highly negative, Lucifer-controlled ETs were so hostile to this that the serpent or snake became synonymous with evil and Ea, the 'Prince of the Earth' became known as the Prince of Darkness. It was nothing more or less than the kind of character assassination, fuelled by lies and propaganda, which we see going on all the time in the modern world.

Those who have read the Adam and Eve story will recall that the serpent, symbolic of Ea, in Bramley's view, did not have the opportunity to persuade them to eat from another tree, the Tree of Life. He was stopped. William Bramley believes that the Brotherhood of the Snake was eventually taken over by the negative ETs and used for their own purposes – to keep the knowledge secret from the mass of the people and to pass it on only to an elite who could be trusted to support the 'great work' of world control and domination. These would be leaders of the people, such as kings and priests, in the civilisations that would follow Atlantis. The aim was to disconnect the conscious level of our being from our higher levels to such an extent that our Earth consciousness would be trapped in the dense physical world and be unable to escape and evolve. Eternal slaves is what they wished to create according to Bramley. I don't know if his interpretations of the Sumer stories are correct in detail, but I have no problem with the idea of an ET involvement on Earth during Atlantis and before. I have long believed that extra-terrestrials seeded the present human form. This is where the different races originally came from, with their many colours and features. Those ETs seeking to help humanity to advance have been seeding human bodies in order to make genetic improvements and to make it easier for the spirit to express its full potential. Put simply, the human form has been subjected to a sort of genetic tug-of-war. I also feel that an organisation, which I will call *the Brotherhood*, has been used over thousands of years to manipulate the human race, and never more so than today.

The extreme negativity which prevailed on the Earth in the latter periods of Atlantis had other implications. Every living form has an energy system, a web of lines linking with the chakras to maintain the flow of lifeforce energies. Acupuncture is based on this understanding. Its practitioners call the lines meridians and the same system applies to planets. A planet has chakras and a grid of energy lines known, depending on your preference, as meridians, ley lines or dragon lines. If you damage and disrupt this energy grid enough you can destroy a planet in the same way that a human body dies when its energy system is sufficiently imbalanced. The basis of acupuncture is to keep the human system in harmony and the physical body healthy. Acupuncture needles are employed to rebalance and redirect the flow of energy. There are certain points, known as acupuncture points, where this can be done most efficiently. So it is with the Earth.

Misuse of knowledge began to threaten this energy grid. Those Atlanteans who were still holding on to the values that brought them here were guided by the higher levels to turn down the power of the energies flowing through and around the planet. The more powerful the energies, the greater was the potential for creation or, should they be misused, for catastrophe. Most Atlanteans were, by now, out of control and the only way to prevent them from destroying the Earth was to reduce the power and potential of the energies available to them. The spacecraft that come to the planet use these energy lines for their power and, if the power is reduced, you reduce the potential for harnessing that power for negative reasons. A piece of channelled information I used in my book *Truth Vibrations* explained it like this:

"In the Atlantean period there were many energies being used and information and knowledge being used which were for particular reasons of safety withdrawn, shall we say, to prevent complete catastrophe, to

prevent total destruction of your planet. One could say these were sort of emergency measures, if you like, to prevent the inhabitants of this planet from an untimely destruction".

I believe that the story of King Arthur and Merlin is, at least in part, a symbolic tale of this turning-down of the energies. I feel these tales relate to Atlanteans and only became legends of knights and kings much later when these kind of stories would have been more readily understood by those they were designed to inform. This also applies to many of the stories in ancient texts which became the Bible. The King Arthur story was, you might say, a sort of parable. The sword Excalibur, I feel, is symbolic of the turning off of those powerful energies – the 'dragon energies' as some people call them. Legend has it that the sword (the energies) was fixed into a stone and only one person had the gifts to remove it. Put another way, only someone with the correct energy pattern can unlock the vibratory key to release the energies which have lain dormant since Atlantis. This process is happening today. 'Excalibur' is being removed and unleashed across the planet. This is being done primarily in Britain and Ireland because this was where the big switch-off was achieved all those thousands of years ago. However, many other locations on the planet are involved, too. The Earth's energy field is now being prepared for its imminent evolution to a higher frequency as the period of Luciferic opportunity comes to an end. The channelled explanation went on:

"As in your human body, there are energy lines around your planet, through your planet, which correspond, I suppose, very much to the acupuncture lines and meridians in your body. Where two lines cross, you create a vortex, a tiny vortex if it's two. The more lines that intersect, the bigger the vortex. Therefore when you have a chakra you have a large vortex of intersecting energy. It is the same with your planet. Where most lines cross there is the biggest vortex. Now you could say that the plexus (network) in and around the Islands you call the British Isles is the hub of the wheel of plexuses and energies which surround your planet. It has acted in other times like a fail-safe device. In order to activate these chakric points upon your planet, the energies must all pass through the central point. They must pass through the heart of the pattern."

The number of those who had the knowledge of this central point and how to close it down were very few. The keys to this point were *"a consciousness pattern, a series of harmonic equations, known only to the keepers of that pattern."*

My belief is that the energies that were switched off, or at least massively turned down, were, in part, the Earth's kundalini energies. These energies in the base chakra, often symbolised by the snake, serpent or dragon, are a seat of our power. The Atlanteans knew how to work with this power but, as with all things, power can be used constructively or destructively. In their later days they chose destruction and the source of their power had to be removed. The suppressing of the kundalini flow obviously had great emotional, physical and mental effects on the Earth as a physical and spiritual entity and the power and knowledge within her aura (the energies we live within and are part of) was consequently diminished. In evolutionary terms, the Earth Spirit and humanity went backwards. At the time that Yeva channelled the information about humanity giving the Luciferic consciousness the chance to re-balance itself, she was also shown a symbolic vision of how this has affected human evolution. She saw the energy stream of evolution going forwards and then suddenly turning back on itself before returning to the starting point, so completing a large loop. It is within that symbolic loop that the period of Luciferic opportunity has unfolded. We are now coming back to the point where it all began in terms of our evolution. When the loop is complete, the period of opportunity will be over and we will continue our evolution without the extreme negative influence of the Luciferic disruption.

Once the harmonic 'key' was turned at the end of Atlantis, the power no longer existed for the imbalanced Atlanteans to destroy everything. The vibratory rate fell and the density of the planet increased. The Earth was falling down the wavelengths of consciousness and disconnecting from a powerful link with higher levels of being. With every fall, the levels of understanding, knowledge and wisdom available to the human race were correspondingly reduced. This, for me, is what is really meant by the Fall of Man. It is the fall down the frequencies of knowledge and wisdom into denser matter. As the fall continued, humanity 'forgot' about Atlantis because we were falling further and further away in consciousness terms from the frequency on which all that happened. With the frequencies rising today, we will be remembering more and more about Atlantis as the fall is reversed and the Earth's kundalini and other energies are re-released.

The behaviour of the Atlanteans and the efforts of the Luciferic consciousness so affected the Earth's energy field that Atlantis was sunk in stages by colossal earthquakes, volcanoes and tidal waves. It could well be that at least the final cataclysms were caused by a rebalancing beam passing across the Earth, which I will explain more fully in a moment. The effect of this 'photon beam', as some people call it, is to rebalance energy fields. If an energy field is fundamentally out of balance the rebalancing process can create staggering physical and mental effects. I'm sure that some kind of nuclear war broke out, too, and that the Earth was also hit during the destruction of Atlantis by a large piece of debris, possibly part of the remains of Maldek. The energies are electromagnetic and different energy fields attract or repel each other. Like attracts like in these circumstances. So, if the Earth's energy field goes through a highly negative phase, it is more likely to attract to itself other negative fields – like the debris careering around the galaxy. I feel that, among the planets, at least the Moon and Venus have 'gone walkabout' before dropping into their present orbits. This would clearly have caused fantastic upheavals as they shattered the balance within the energy fields of other planets and star systems. This series of incredible geological events in several distinct phases caused, no doubt, by a variety of reasons, ended the civilisation called Atlantis. Researchers have found evidence of a 10,000ft uplift in the Andes about ten thousand years ago. This is because whole mountain ranges soared from the surface of the Earth during these periods. There was a magnetic pole shift and a tilt of the Earth on its axis. This sent a fantastic tidal wave around the planet. The giant crystal at the centre of the Atlantean power system was lost under the ocean and it is this which might be creating the strange phenomenon known as the Bermuda Triangle. From time to time, it might open a gateway from one dimension to another. Other planets of this solar system which were highly imbalanced went through similar upheavals and all hell broke loose across a wide area. It seems to me that the Earth fell out of alignment, in some way, with the universal energy grid.

The turning down of the energy points and the vibratory 'fall' trapped the Atlantean consciousness within the Earth's frequencies and many who could have escaped chose, for various reasons, to stay and carry on the work. To do this, they had to begin the cycle of incarnating from the Earth's non-physical frequencies into the human form. This process included the volunteers who were still on the path and those who had either been led astray by the Luciferic Consciousness or were aspects of that consciousness. Other volunteers could not stand the falling frequencies and left before it was too late. The Earth's vibration and atmosphere became much denser and the light/dark struggle would manifest in a different way. I am not sure exactly why, but from now on the ET presence on Earth, both negative and positive, would take another form. Most of their influence was spread by affecting human consciousness through planting ideas, beliefs, and thought patterns. I do think that they still came in their spacecraft to observe, support, or manipulate depending on their state of being, but it was mostly done in much more subtle ways and was very different from the Atlantis and pre-Atlantis times. Since the end of Atlantis, those who continued to work for the evolution of the planet and humanity have been incarnating to spread the spiritual truths and prepare the World for today's great time of change. As a channelled communication said:

"There are many of you for whom the Earth is not your indigenous evolutionary home, shall we say. There are many of you on this planet who come from other spheres of evolution. I think these have been called 'star children' by some of your writers, that is a good enough expression. More evolved beings came to your planet and manifested on your planet in Atlantean times. This was the biggest impulse in bringing the new knowledge into Atlantis which caused it to grow into the civilisation that it was. New knowledge was brought into this system from universal sources from highly evolved spirits, bringing knowledge into the planet. And you're going to bring it back, basically."

A plan was set in motion to restore the Earth after Atlantis. This plan had three main motivations:

To help the Luciferic consciousness to re-harmonise before its 'opportunity' period came to an end,

To seek to protect human consciousness from further imbalance,

To check the fall of the Earth's energy field to ever lower vibrations.

This final point is crucial to what is happening on the planet today. Creation is self-balancing. You can push it out of balance for a certain period but then it kicks back to find harmony. This loop of opportunity for the Luciferic consciousness had a definite time scale and now, in the lifetimes of our generations, it is coming to a close. It is time for Planet Earth to return to its original evolutionary road.

Everything from the inside of an atom to a universe is in orbit around a central point. Some researchers believe that our solar system, together with a much wider area, is in orbit around the star system known as the Pleiades. According to the writer Paul Otto Hesse, this orbit is centred in particular around Alcyone, the brightest star in the Pleiades. Some people say it takes 24,000 years for our sun to complete such an orbit. Hesse believes that it is from Alcyone and the Pleiades that the Photon Belt I have mentioned is projected. It is a beam of highly charged energy particles that re-balances and re-synchronises all energy fields that pass through it. I use the term Photon Belt for simplicity, but that term, and the location of Alcyone, are Hesse's research, not mine. I know it only as a synchronisation beam and have no idea of its exact composition nor from where it emanates. But the effect is the same: Fantastic transformation.

As the beam is a circle, each orbit of our solar system around Alcyone (if that is correct) possibly takes us through the beam twice. It is estimated that it takes around 2,000 years to pass completely through it. No matter what state of imbalance a planet may be experiencing, the passage through the photon beam will re-balance it at the vibratory level most appropriate to its evolution. The vital point, however, is that the more imbalanced a planet's energy field is when it enters that beam, the more disruption and upheaval will be caused in the re-balancing process. It is that potentially cataclysmic upheaval that the volunteer consciousness has been trying to avoid by working to check the gathering imbalances caused by the Luciferic consciousness. You can see, given the potential consequences, what an act of love it has been for the human mind to offer this opportunity to that consciousness.

The planet has already experienced the great upheaval which marked the end of Atlantis and it could happen again if we don't flood the Earth's energy field with love. The Photon Belt acts as a sort of harvester, giving the opportunity to those who are ready to move out of this level of existence to graduate to a higher one. During the Atlantean period it is possible that it re-balanced the Earth's energy field.

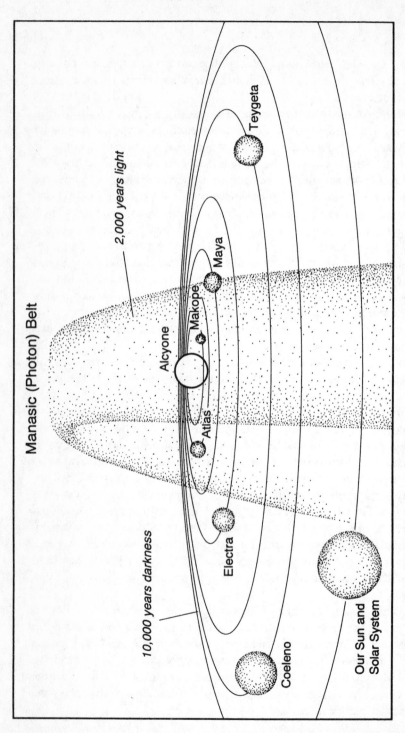

THE PLEIDIAN SYSTEM: Alcyone is the brightest star in the constellation of Pleiades. Our sun takes 24,000 years to complete a full revolution around Alcyone.

The Earth, while being rebalanced, did not herself take that evolutionary leap because it was not the right time. She could not have done so, anyway, with her energy field weakened by the switching off of certain key energy flows. Now the time is right for the Earth to make that evolutionary step and return to where she was before the Luciferic opportunity period began. In other words, the evolutionary 'loop' is being completed and the Earth is returning to her original evolutionary path. I think the same is true of the solar system and further afield. The Luciferic opportunity is coming to a close. The pass across the photon beam which is happening now will, I feel, be potentially more far-reaching in its effect than it was even during Atlantis. This time the whole energy field of Planet Earth is being 'harvested' and it is taking a massive step up in its evolution. Those who do not do the same will not be able to incarnate on the Earth after this process is complete because the Earth will be operating on too high a frequency for them to exist here until they have raised their own vibrations to match those of this planet.

The idea of this re-balancing beam was identified by the Maya people more than a thousand years ago. When the Mayan Civilisation was at the height of its powers in Central America between around 435AD and 850AD, they were well ahead of today's mainstream science in their understanding of Creation. This was because they, too, were, in part, an incarnation of the advanced volunteer consciousness. They would have channelled other frequencies and possibly interacted with space visitors. They knew of these beam cycles crossing the Earth and produced a system of numbers and symbols to measure these periods. According to the calculations the Maya left behind on their magnificent pyramids and temples, the current 'great cycle' of the Earth's evolution began in 3113BC and will end in the year 2012. This corresponds with the prophecies of others such as Nostradamus who foresaw enormous change in this period, as one era of human evolution passed and another made its entrance.

The year 2012 is when those who follow the Mayan calculations believe that Planet Earth will be re-synchronised. Different people put different time scales on these things, but they all agree on the basic period. My feeling is that the 'window' of time in which we will see the most dramatic change is between the 1990s and circa 2030. I will give more details of the effects of this period when we reach the present day in our chronological story. I felt it was worth mapping out the basic themes, however, at this early stage because it will help to put into context much of what our story will describe. All over the Universe are other highly-evolved civilisations working to help humanity and the Earth. Some of their number come into incarnation, others travel here in spacecraft, and still others operate as channelled communicators to Earth people. These other civilisations have evolved to the point where they can think as individuals or link their minds collectively, so accessing all the knowledge and wisdom available in the sum total of the parts. Guiding the overall operation is a Galactic and Universal consciousness which is given many names by channellers. This is the consciousness which is guiding the Earth and those in incarnation who are here to serve the Universe by serving humanity and the planet. That consciousness will, in turn, be guided by the Source.

Against this line-up of love, however, are aspects of the Luciferic consciousness which also manifest in physical bodies, ETs, and as channelled communicators. These are guided by their version of a Universal consciousness which is in opposition to the Source and seeks to undermine the efforts of all those who wish to open the prison door for both humanity and the Earth. For many thousands of years, the evolution of Planet Earth has been dominated by the struggle between these two states of being, harmony and disharmony. Thanks to the re-balancing beam there can be only one winner – harmony. But this does not diminish the horrors which disharmony has visited, upon the world.

2

Collective Amnesia

THE Earth took a long time to recover from the cataclysms and, even when the physical surface began to heal, it was now a very different world.

Gone was the knowledge that built Atlantis, because the frequency of consciousness that could be accessed on Earth was much lower and more primitive than it had been. The energy field had been re-balanced but the energies had come to rest, as it were, at a much lower frequency than they had once enjoyed. In vibratory terms it was like incarnating into treacle. It was even more difficult for those highly-evolved minds who were still working for the restoration of the planet to manifest that understanding while encased in a dense physical body. Their bodies were now denser than they had been in Atlantis and the limitations were subsequently greater than they had been used to. The power and potential of the energies around the planet were similarly curtailed. All this made the task of those incarnating to help the Earth immeasurably more demanding.

The events at the end of Atlantis had attracted large numbers of beings to this area of Creation to help with the plan. The Earth's energy field had to be prepared for the next crossing of the Photon Belt when it would return to its original evolutionary level and beyond. Other volunteers began to incarnate on to the Earth. But this dense physical frequency and many others continued to be dominated by the Luciferic disruption. That consciousness as expressed through negative ETs had been largely removed from the physical level of the planet by the rebalancing process but now it began to stimulate disharmony again. The lower frequency made this easier, if anything, and disharmony in the planet's energy field gathered pace as the Luciferic consciousness entered the last stage of its 'opportunity' period – an opportunity it showed no signs of taking. I once had a vision of the Earth which took the form of a ball of glass like the ones you see hanging from the ceiling in discos and dance halls. As the ball spun, it was reflecting light in all directions. I believe this was symbolic of the role the Earth plays. But, instead of sending out light and love, she has been generating negative energy. She has become like a negativity production unit which is imbalancing and holding back the evolution of the solar system and all that is currently entering the Photon Belt and preparing to evolve. This is being made more difficult by the drag and disharmony of the Earth and the frequencies that surround her. This is creating vibratory pressures and tensions which are reaching a critical point. One piece of channelled information I used in *Truth Vibrations* said:

" The Universe needs the life the Earth brings forth and the whole must be preserved. It is not for you alone that we do this work. There has always been an order in the way the planets have been governed. Man has not understood the linkages which bind everything together."

This is another reason why the volunteer consciousness is focusing on Planet Earth. What happens here affects a much wider area. All planets and stars are connected by a web of energy lines to a universal grid. If a chakra or pulse point on this grid is damaged or starts to generate imbalanced energies, it affects everything connected to that grid. These can eventually affect other frequencies and the imbalance can grow like a cancer. It has become clear to me over these years of my spiritual reawakening that, if the Earth goes on being abused, so much negative energy will be created that the consequences for the wider Universe could be very unpleasant as it goes through its evolutionary leap.

The imbalances and density of the Earth affect humanity in many ways. It is worth repeating here that not all of our consciousness incarnates into a physical body and becomes subject to its severe limitations. The higher levels of our consciousness (higher self) stay on a non-physical level and guide the lower self through an incarnation. The higher self knows the lifeplan – what we hope to achieve and experience during that life. If, however, we lose touch with the higher self, Mission Control, we become dominated by the information coming in through the eyes and the ears and we are prey to the thought patterns directed at this level by the Luciferic consciousness. These work particularly on the emotions and the ego and, once the Lucifer patterns have control of those, they can, by affecting our behaviour, cause untold pain and destruction. This is what has happened to the human race. We can come into incarnation with the best of intentions but, once we look out through our eyes and become subjected to all the information this level constantly bombards us with, we can forget why we are here and act in ways that are the exact opposite of what we intended before incarnation. This is especially so if the kundalini energies are suppressed because, in that state of being, the other chakras are not linked powerfully to the physical level. Thus, the physical is not fully connected to our higher levels. (The source of the kundalini energy is the base of the spine, the seat of our sexuality and of harmonious relationship.)

It can be even worse if a higher self is working from one of the non-physical frequencies still dominated by that Luciferic consciousness. In these cases, you have a misguided lower self and a misguided higher self. There are also direct incarnations of the Lucifer consciousness. Look back through history and around the world today and you will see many examples of this. The imbalances of the Earth, its density and a suppressed or imbalanced kundalini flow, make the connection and communication between higher and lower self much more difficult during an incarnation. With the influence of 'Mission Controls' getting weaker, lower selves come under the control of eyes and ears information. If Lucifer can manipulate that information and fill the human mind with negative thought patterns, it follows that he could encourage humanity to act in ways that generate yet more negative energy into the ocean of consciousness in which we exist. More negative energy increases the power of the Luciferic consciousness. We can feel these energies when we meet someone and say, 'Hey, I got bad vibes from him'. Or, perhaps, we go into a house and say, 'I don't like it in here – it's eerie'. At these times we are feeling the non-physical energy generated by a person or by others in the past. What we call atmosphere is really the energy, negative or positive, generated by human beings or non-physical entities. The atmosphere we describe at football matches, for instance, is made up of the energies generated by the crowd.

Since the end of Atlantis, the imbalances have been fuelled both by the thought patterns transmitted by the Luciferic consciousness and by the negative energies generated by humanity. As a result, the Earth has become subjected to an ever more serious negative imbalance which has led to the state of the world we see today.

Lucifer has sought to control the information and thought patterns of the dense physical level to such an extent that whoever incarnated on to the Earth would become subjected to those patterns and to the influence of the people already affected by them. A simple example of this is can be found in parents controlled or strongly influenced by the Lucifer thought patterns who indoctrinate their children to think in the same way. Once control of the human mind has been largely accomplished at the collective level, each successive generation has faced pressure to conform to that way of thinking.

Every species has, as I have outlined, a collective mind, a level to which all minds in incarnation are linked. It has been shown that, once a certain number of a species learns to do something new, suddenly other members of the same species are able to do the same thing without being shown. This so-called 'Hundredth Monkey Syndrome' is the collective mind at work. Once enough individual minds start thinking in a particular way, their thought patterns become strong enough in the collective mind for other individuals to access that information. That's how the Hundredth Monkey Syndrome works. With Lucifer transmitting thought patterns into the collective mind and using billions of dense physical bodies over the centuries to do the same, it is not difficult to see how the illusions and misunderstandings of humanity have arisen and become so powerful.

There were three tasks which those who had come to the Earth needed to perform in order to restore harmony. One was to create a temporary energy grid on the planet to replace the one devastated during Atlantis; the second was to restore and re-open that Atlantis energy system when the time was right and re-awaken the closed-down energies before the Earth's evolutionary leap during the present pass of the Photon Belt; and the third was to give human beings as much information as possible to help them to remember who they really were and what they had come to do. If it was difficult for humanity's higher selves to communicate with them, this problem could be by-passed, to some extent, by using those who did maintain a good connection to bring information directly to this dense physical level. Also, everyone who changed their thinking in the light of this information would be sending thought patterns into the collective mind to challenge the Lucifer domination.

These efforts were made more difficult by the way the frequency had fallen and by the nature of the imbalances it was subject to. On this frequency were negative emotions and mental states of a scale and severity that these evolved volunteers had never experienced directly before. If the personnel were to be capable of playing their part in those generations at the end of the 20th century, they had to have mastered, to a large extent, the emotions, temptations, illusions and fears so prevalent on the Earth. If they did not, they would be unable to do what was required and the transition period would be even more traumatic and difficult than it already promised to be. As well as coming into incarnation to pass on information and work on the energy grid, these beings also had to be put through lives that would give them experience of some very unpleasant emotions. Only in this way could they learn to overcome them. Sometimes they would have lives in which they worked almost exclusively on the energy system and on the spreading of information; sometimes they would have lives designed primarily to experience negative emotions and overcome them. Mostly their lives were a combination of both.

Over the thousands of years since the destruction of Atlantis, those working for the restoration of the planet have been incarnating over and over again and, in that process, have been amassing karmic debt which has had to be balanced out. Some became so affected by the pressures of this level that they no longer followed the path they had embarked upon after Atlantis. They came to free the prisoners and ended up in jail themselves, trapped by the pressures and desires of the dense physical world and undermined by the Luciferic consciousness which seeks to stop the volunteers, in particular. Most of them have been historically anonymous, living simple lives and being guided to work on the energy system. Many of the great stone circles and the standing stones of the world were built either by, or under the direction of, these people. Pyramids and the stones are the physical manifestation of the work that went on thousands of years ago to construct a sort of makeshift energy grid to keep the Earth ticking over until the Atlantean one could be reactivated in our lifetimes. They would have sensed the energies and been guided to do what was required because the energy imbalances at that time were not as great as they would later become and the connection with the higher self would have been potentially more powerful. Also every effort is made by other levels to make the higher self/lower self connection of certain key people as strong as it can possibly be when particular tasks need to be achieved.

Pyramid geometry is such that it has a very significant effect on energy flows, negative or positive depending on how they are used, while the stone circles and standing stones act like fuse boxes and acupuncture needles receiving energies from the universal grid and rebalancing the flows. If you look back at any civilisation which was more evolved than the rest of the world, you will be looking at either a group incarnation of those who volunteered to help the Earth or at the effects of spaceship landings or channelled information which passed on the knowledge. That doesn't mean that the volunteers were perfect. They were subject to the pressures of this world, also. And what is perfect, anyway? But they were in close enough synchronisation with their higher self for knowledge to reach this level which helped the earth and human understanding.

When I say that the volunteer consciousness incarnated into certain civilisations, I don't mean that every member of that nation or race was that consciousness incarnate. Only some of them. These were the ones who accessed the information and understanding from higher levels which either helped those civilisations to evolve very quickly or challenged the political, economic and religious dogma of their day. Around them there would have been people who ignored them or killed them for their 'heresy' as well as those who listened and supported their views on how a society could best prosper in peace. That is the situation in its most simplistic form. But, of course, it is more complex than that. Some of the volunteer consciousness has become imbalanced and is either not working for the good of the planet or is actively working against it. Some of the Luciferic consciousness will have been so affected by its experiences that it has rejected that negative influence. In most cases, people are affected by both. No-one is all good or all negative. The question is which part of us is dominating our behaviour and to what degree?

Extra-terrestrials continued to come to the Earth in this post-Atlantis period, and were considered to be gods by the Earth people. This is not surprising when you imagine what it must have been like for the primitive Earth people to be confronted by spacecraft and their occupants. We should not underestimate the scale of the influence on human evolution on all levels, positive and negative, by other civilisations in the Universe. When you look through the Bible and other ancient texts you can see what appear to be spacecraft described. The Book of Ezekiel is a prime example and, indeed, there is an analysis of this called *The Space Ships Of Ezekiel* by Josef F. Blumrich, a former chief of systems layout at NASA. His work strongly suggests that a number of biblical texts are describing spacecraft. Analysis of many ancient writings and the artwork of peoples all over the world also appears to contain descriptions of such craft and their occupants, who were thought to be 'gods from the sky'. Ancient Indian Sanskrit texts speak of gods who fought in aircraft and certainly the Book of Ezekiel leaves you in little doubt of what was being described:

"Now as I looked upon the living creatures, I saw four wheels upon the ground, one by each of the living creatures, with their four faces.
The appearance of the wheels and their composition was like the colour of shiny amber; and all four wheels had one likeness; and their appearance and their composition was like a wheel in the middle of a wheel...
"And when the living creatures went, the wheels went with them; and when the living creatures were lifted up from the earth, the wheels were lifted up.
"And the appearance of the sky upon the heads of the living creatures was reflected as the colour of the terrible crystal stretched over their heads above...
"And when they went, I heard the noise of their wings, like the noise of great waters, as the voice of the Almighty, like the din of an army. When they stood still, they lowered their wings. And there was a voice from the crystal covering that was over their heads when they stood and had let down their wings."

Ezekiel 1: 1-25

The Babylonians had a god called Oannes, a fishtailed amphibious being who, according to their legends, came to Earth to start a civilisation. Some people look at the primitive way of life on the planet during these periods and laugh at the idea of highly-evolved spacecraft landing here. But people from the computerised, technological, western culture today visit parts of the world that still live more or less as the ancients did. No-one finds that funny or hard to accept. The only difference between that and what I am suggesting about spacecraft is that, in the extra-terrestrial case, the technological culture visiting a more primitive one is interplanetary rather than intercontinental.

We will pick up the story of what happened to humanity after

Atlantis in the fertile land between the Euphrates and Tigris rivers. This area became known as Mesopotamia and is now Iraq. Here the Sumerian people settled and were supported by visitations from many extra-terrestrial peoples, some to help, some to exploit. Official history dates this period from around 4,000BC, but it was probably much earlier. The Sumerians were said to have built the first cities of the post-Atlantis era, but there were many other civilisations before that. One was in Israel, around Jericho, for sure. According to Sumerian records preserved on baked bricks, they themselves came to the area with a knowledge of writing, the arts, agriculture and metalwork. I am sure that the knowledge contained in their writings and artifacts came to them from earlier civilisations that history hasn't yet recorded. The Sumerians used their agricultural skills and the rich silt left by the rivers in times of flood, to grow two crops of wheat each year. A culture developed that was, as far as we know, well ahead of most of the planet at that time. A library of more than 30,000 written tablets was created and the discovery of some of these has given us an understanding of the Sumerian background and history. Some of the symbols found on Sumerian artifacts correspond with those in the crop circles that appear in the fields of southern England and elsewhere today.

The two main cities of Mesopotamia were Eridu, the capital of Sumer, and Nippur to the North, the capital of Akkad, which was inhabited by a Semitic race. The two cities had very different religious beliefs and cultures. Eridu worshipped the God, Ea, while En-lil was the God of Nippur. Later the Arabian word, Allah, would devolve from En-lil, as would the Hebrew word for God, El, who was also to become the Christian God. I have no doubt that Ea and En-lil were extra-terrestrials from that earlier period we talked about. By now they had entered Sumerian legends as 'gods'. Extra-terrestrials and the psychic channellings and visions which people experienced were the foundations of the religions that would follow, right up to the present day. Not all the gods came from these sources. Some were just made up or the product of confused minds but most were ET or psychic in their origins.

Look at the implications for the Bible and other 'holy' books of the themes emerging in our story so far. The judgmental god so widely quoted in the Old Testament and other ancient texts, who threatens to bring horrors upon human beings if they don't do as he tells them, merely reflects the attitudes of the negative ETs or channelled entities. They are not the words of God but those of the extra-terrestrials and channelled entities who were thought to be gods. Go to church and worship an ET! The idea that God created humans in his own image would describe perfectly the seeding of the human form as we know it by extra-terrestrials considered to be gods.

I stress here that, when truths were passed on, they were communicated in ways which the people of the time could understand. From the symbolic explanations of thousands of years ago have come the religious dogmas as the symbolism has been taken literally and added to or changed around. When ancient texts say clearly, *'This story is a parable'*, religions accept the tale as symbolic but many take everything else in the text literally. In fact, most of these texts are symbolic and told in parable form. I use a lot of symbolic explanations in my books which relate to what people today experience and easily identify with. It has always been like that. So there are still truths in the Bible and many other ancient texts despite what the religions have done to destroy and debase them. But these truths and the mathematical codes they also contain will never be understood if they continue to be taken literally rather than symbolically; nor while religions continue to proclaim that everything written in them is one hundred per cent accurate and the infallible word of God when a goodly proportion is clearly invented claptrap passed on from one people to another through the centuries.

Religious dogma and myth have been used very successfully either to suppress understanding or to twist the truth sufficiently to turn something positive into something negative. The story of Adam and Eve is an example. It has been used to undermine women (Eve tempts Adam in the story to eat from the Tree of Knowledge against the command of God, and so evil starts with the creation of women). It has also been used to justify the belief that we are all born sinners (our ancestral lines are all supposed to go back genetically to the original 'sinners', Adam and Eve). This nonsense is still blindly followed today to justify some terrible behaviour. My goodness. God help us!

To weave a way through this minefield we have to look at the symbolism in the Sumerian stories and other ancient texts but not take them all literally. Even the symbolism is multi-dimensional. I don't believe the symbolism of the snake, for example, relates entirely to the Garden of Edinnu or Eden. I feel that the snake or

serpent has been used as a symbol for many things. The Mesopotamian culture had a serpent-god called Ningishzida represented by
two intertwining snakes. These are possibly symbolic of the two
opposing forces, positive-negative, male-female, in balance within
the kundalini energy as it rises through the central channel to
connect and empower the chakras on the physical level. Appropri-
ately, though somewhat ironically, the symbol of the medical
profession to this day is an intertwining snake. The symbol of
modern medicine represents knowledge of the physical body and
the human energy field known thousands of years ago, but now
rejected by the very profession which has that knowledge in its
symbol!

Serpents and similar symbols have also been used throughout
ancient cultures to represent the Goddess or female polarity of
Creation. The earlier concepts of the Trinity had a female symbol
as one of the triangle of 'gods' while the more enlightened religions
speak of a Father/Mother God to highlight the need for male-
female balance within both ourselves and the whole. The Christian
version of this idea of a Trinity – Father, Son and Holy Ghost –
does not recognise the feminine and that has been reflected in its
attitude to women over the centuries. All the ancient and more
spiritually enlightened cultures like the Sumerians, the Egyptians,
the Greeks, the native Americans (Indians), the Australian abori-
gines and many of the East, knew of the importance of the kundalini and had initiations, often very tough ones, to speed the
smooth activation and empowerment of these energies. The snake
and serpent were, more often than not, a representation of this.
Similarly, their belief in resurrection or rebirth was often symbolised by the snake shedding its skin as it moved from one state of
being into another.

There were some periods of peace in Sumer, but it was also
plagued by inter-city battles and, gradually, the civilisation de-
cayed and disappeared. This was to be a running theme through
human evolution – the desire to impose beliefs or to steal the
benefits of an advanced culture, causing war after war and,
thereby, destroying what human ingenuity and the volunteer consciousness had created. It is also the case, as we will discuss more
thoroughly later, that if you wish to control people and stop them
evolving spiritually then causing conflict between them is an excel-
lent way to achieve that aim. The culture of the Sumerians was to
influence others who began to develop in the region we call the

Middle East. Sumerian beliefs and knowledge found their way to the Egyptians, Babylonians, Assyrians, Hebrews and, later, the Greeks. In turn, the Greeks would influence the Romans and the Sumerians could fairly be said to have been the foundation of much that would follow. Writing and such architectural constructions as the arch and the dome first appear with the Sumerians in the post-Atlantis period although these probably go back further to pre-Sumer times. The Hebrews inherited many of their own beliefs from Mesopotamia and Egypt and these have been passed on through the generations as Judaism and, eventually, Christianity. The idea of the Sabbath comes from the Sumerians as does the Great Flood, the Fall of Man and the laws that have been associated with Moses. One Sumerian tablet records the story of Creation which, in all its main themes, is the same as that reported in Genesis.

The God myths, largely, though not entirely, the result of ET and psychic activities, were already well underway by Sumer times. Another Sumerian tablet tells the story of Bel, which means the Son of God. Bel was to become the saviour-myth figure of Babylon and would be known to the Hebrews as Baal. Bel, the Sumerian son of God, was the Lord Christ and redeemer in Babylonian thought. They believed he had died and risen again to ensure their salvation. Heard that somewhere before? The Babylonians performed a Passion drama and sang hymns that were very close to the Passion plays and services of the later Christians. Bel was the second in a trinity of gods – Ea, the Father; Bel, the Son, and Anu, the Holy Spirit. It was the custom to sacrifice a lamb to the gods because, as one tablet says, *"The lamb is the substitute for humanity."* What is it that the Bible tells us? *"...the Lamb of God which taketh away the sins of the world."*

The 'lamb' of the Bible is said to be Jesus, but that's just a piece of myth-recycling. The basic story of Bel and other key elements of this Sumerian and Babylonian belief-system were taken back to Judea by the Jews after they were freed from captivity in Babylon. They then found their way into the texts that make up the Old Testament and, through them, into the New Testament. So we have the Bible talking of Jesus as the Lamb of God dying so that our sins can be forgiven or, as they were saying thousands of years earlier in Mesopotamia during their animal sacrifices, *'The lamb is the substitute for humanity'*. One Sumerian tablet even records the story of how Sargon, the King of the Semites, was hidden by his mother in a basket made from bulrushes on the bank of the Euphrates, a tale attributed in the Bible to Moses. As we will see, the whole basis of the Jewish, Christian and many other religions comes from stories inherited over the centuries which each religion attributes to its own particular saviour-god. A number of these stories and myths will be symbolic of actual events and eternal truths but their meaning, in most cases, has become so changed, twisted or embellished that the understanding has been lost.

I am not sure how much direct ET involvement went on in Sumer. I want to see more information before I decide what I feel was happening. Obviously this part of the book, in terms of ET involvement, has to be a hypothesis, although one based on much research by a number of people. It is possible that ETs were still making themselves known to the population as a whole, or it could be they were interacting only with certain groups or individuals. But I don't think it is always as simple as ETs manifesting physically. I feel they operate mostly on other frequencies of reality which allow them to be seen only by those who can psychically tune into them. They would certainly have been working through human consciousness and channellers, I would say, and having a considerable influence on events.

What I do feel on the balance of the evidence I have seen and my own intuition, is that the principle of initiating people into the eternal truths began to be misused from at least this Sumer period onwards and probably much earlier. If you remember, the channelling in the last chapter talked about the "Guardians of the Light" in Atlantis being given the knowledge of how to use and harness the energies. This knowledge was kept secret because of the potential for devastation if it was misused. At that time this initiation process was used with the best of intent. This process was, however, to become infiltrated under the influence of the Luciferic consciousness and slowly, but surely, it spawned the enormous network of secret societies we see today, all with similar terms, symbols, and initiation proceedures. This network I will call the Brotherhood.

I stress here that I am not suggesting all secret societies from this moment on were of negative, manipulative, intent. Many continued to use the cover of secrecy in the centuries that followed, to pass on spiritual knowledge which was being systematically destroyed in the outside world, and to speak openly about it would have been tantamount to suicide. The Brotherhood, where used to

communicate the spiritual truths for the good of humanity in line
with its original purpose, has made a vital contribution to keeping
those truths alive through some very dark times. So it is no
contradiction that some great people who have served humanity
well have been involved in Brotherhood secret societies, while the
Brotherhood has also been used to manipulate humanity ap-
pallingly. It depends who is in control of the secret society at a
particular time. What I most strongly contend, however, is that
from now onwards there was a gradual takeover of the Brotherhood initiation process, until it became an overwhelmingly negative influence on humanity and an enormously effective vehicle for
the Luciferic consciousness. I shall be charting this takeover
through the book and highlighting its fundamental effect today on
everyone's lives. The difference between the original Brotherhood
and the Luciferic version is one of intent and method. The original
passed on truths, or what were genuinely perceived to be truths, to
those it believed would use the knowledge wisely; the Luciferic
version gives a twisted and manipulated version of the truths to
those it believes can be trusted to continue its ambitions to control
the world.

The Sumerian civilisation expanded and the famous city of Ur
was built around 3,500BC. Later, an event of some kind occurred
which altered the course of the Euphrates and forced the people to
move North to the river settlement known as Babylon, which
means the Gate of the Gods. Internal strife weakened them and
eventually the Amorites conquered the region and brought together Sumer and Akkad to form Babylonia. The Amorites were a
Semitic race, a branch of which became the Hebrews. King Ham-
murabi became the ruler of what was to be known as Babylonia
and he instigated a system of laws and justice that were to be
adapted for their own use by the Hebrews, Greeks, and Romans.
Education was available to all and everyone had the opportunity to
learn to read and write. There were libraries and universities.

It is important to appreciate, as we look at where present-day
values and beliefs originated, that nothing is new. It is all inherited
from, or influenced by, what has happened in the past. To say that
the beliefs of Christianity were new 2,000 years ago is simply
ridiculous. Even the Christian ceremony called the Eucharist, the
eating of the body and the drinking of the blood, originates from
the days of cannibalism. Today, Christians eat bread and drink red
wine to symbolise Christ's body and blood. In the ceremonies

from which this originated, they ate and drank the real thing in human and animal sacrifices! The Greeks called it *the Eucharistia*.

The Assyrians travelled three hundred miles to the south to invade and conquer Babylonia around 1280BC and, over the next 200 years or so, they extended their empire across to the Mediterranean. After a period of internal war, the Assyrians invaded Egypt, but this campaign so exhausted them physically and financially that they were conquered by the Chaldeans who moved their centre to Babylon. The best known of the Chaldean kings was Nebuchadnezzar who reigned from 604 to 561BC and it was he who invaded through Judea to take command of Egypt. Jews were taken captive and removed to Babylon where they were to have access to the stories of Bel, the Son of God, and the other Mesopotamian beliefs I have been talking about.

The next conquerors on the scene were the Persians who took Babylonia in 539BC. The Jews believed these invaders had been sent by their God, Jehovah, to free them from captivity when, in fact, like so many other peoples, the Persians merely wished to extend their empire and steal all the booty they could find. The Jews had supported the Persians in their attack on Babylon and were allowed to return to Judea. They took with them the stories and beliefs they had heard in Babylon and this was to be a great influence on the emergence of both the Jewish and Christian religions. The Persians had a belief in one God in contrast to the many-god religions that abounded among those people who believed that different gods were responsible for every facet of nature and the many ET and other 'gods' which became myth figures over the centuries. So, when all those 'gods' became fused into the one God, he was an amalgamation of all those different myths and beliefs. No wonder the Bible is so contradictory.

By 500BC the Persians controlled an area from Egypt to the borders of India. Communications improved with the building of the royal road from near the Persian Gulf almost to the Aegean Sea and Greeks began to travel south to visit Babylon. There they heard the stories of Bel and others and met with people from India and Syria. Their knowledge and beliefs were exchanged and the fusion of myths continued apace.

3

A Brotherhood of Clans

EGYPT was another major influence on the pre-Christian world. The name means 'black land' and refers to the silt left by the flooding Nile.

Like Sumer, this civilisation grew from settlements on a major river where the fertility of the soil would ensure that there was enough to eat. Researchers believe the land was settled before 3,000BC and developed into a system of Pharaoh dynasties and dictatorships. I feel the Egyptian civilization goes back thousands of years earlier than this and new research is supporting that contention. There are some who believe that extra-terrestrials were very active in this region, at least in the early days. I have no problem in accepting that the culture was seriously influenced, either by legends and myths originating from ET activity, or by the direct appearance on some level of spacecraft and their occupants, probably both. What form this interaction took, I'm not sure, and again ETs operate on many other levels of reality. If you look at many of the statues, artwork, and face make-up from early Egypt and Mesopotamia, they often emphasise large eyes. There are several civilisations elsewhere in the Universe which have very large eyes when compared to ours. I am sure that some Egyptian 'gods' were extra-terrestrial in origin and the Egyptians said that these 'gods' went into the sky in their flying boats.

There is a view among some researchers which says that ETs, some with a human-like form, came regularly to the Earth in these ancient times and began the tradition of god-kings in many civilisations which, in Egypt, manifested as the Pharaohs. It is said that these kings were the human extension of negative extra-terrestrial control and that the whole idea of a monarchy came from their wish to manipulate humanity. The Pharaohs and kings were, according to this theory, persuaded that they were different from the rest of humanity and the representatives of the gods (ETs) on earth. In fact, this belief system contends, the monarchs were puppets being used by some space people to keep the masses in ignorance and spiritual imprisonment. The monarchs, too, were conned and indoctrinated, it is said. I don't know and have no way of knowing if there is any truth in this, but I offer it to you as information and make of it what you will. I've put it all on the back burner for now with a great deal else, but it makes sense to me.

One highly significant Pharaoh was Amenophis IV. About five years into his reign he adopted the name Khu-n-aten and is now known as Akhenaton. He abolished idols and the traditional multi-god religion and moved the capital from Thebes to a new city in Middle Egypt called El-Amarna. A Brotherhood temple was built there in the shape of a cross and he established the simple worship of the Sun God, Aten. Perhaps he realised the true significance of the Sun as a source of knowledge and guidance, or possibly he was used by the Brotherhood to create a new one-god religion. Some researchers see him as a tool of the Brotherhood infiltrators who misled his people. Maybe he was. I don't know the truth about him. Anyone can be manipulated; that is particularly true when you have left this physical level and can no longer challenge what is said and done in your name. Look at the man we call Jesus! And as I keep stressing, secret societies can be used for good or ill – it depends on who is in control and what society they are operating in. The French Resistance in the Second World War was a secret society in a sense. I don't believe it is wise to be black and white on this as some researchers are. For instance, I believe that Akhenaton was right, there is only one God, one overall consciousness, but that doesn't mean that I agree with everything else he believed. We have to be selective and free ourselves from rigid dogma.

What I do feel is that at least after the time of Akenaton the infiltration of the Brotherhood and it's expansion did gather pace. When Akhenaton died in about 1362BC his successors moved the court back to Thebes and reinstated the multi-god religions. One successor had a preference for the cult of the god Amen or Amun and he changed his name from Tutankhaten to Tutankhamun. He was to become world-famous thousands of years later when his tomb was uncovered in the Valley of the Kings at Luxor. Akhenaton was to be branded a heretic. While the court was moved back to Thebes, the Brotherhood and its Mystery School of secret initiations stayed put. It used the temple built by Akhenaton as its headquarters and, in doing so, broke away from the state hierarchy. From El-Amarna, agents of the Brotherhood were sent out to set up other branches far and wide. I believe that from this point, the Egyptian Brotherhood was probably working with less than positive intent and the expansion of the infiltrated, Luciferic version would now begin to spread its influence and manipulation. Each of the Brotherhood priests at El-Amarna had a bald spot and wore a cord around his robe, tied at the loins. This mode of appearance was later adopted by many other orders such as the Franciscan monks in Christian times. The Mystery Schools were a vehicle to pass on the secret knowledge for positive and negative intent and for the use of hallucinogenic drugs, sexual rites, and human sacrifice was not unknown either, depending on who controlled them. Mind control techniques were well understood.

Offshoots of the Brotherhood began to emerge, particularly from these Egyptian and Babylonian times. Each had the same secret codes, symbols and initiations. No one in these secret societies is allowed to know what is going on at the level above them and this is an extremely effective means of manipulation which has been used through the ages. Such organisations continue to this day with names like the Freemasons, Knights Templar, the Order of the Quest, the Knights of Malta, the Jesuits, the Round Table and countless others. The Brotherhood is now at the elite level, under the control of the negative consciousness. The names may have changed and the number increased enormously since ancient times, but the agenda remains the same. I am not saying that every member of these societies is knowingly working against the good of humanity. Certainly not. Most of them will not have a clue about how their society is being used. What I am saying is that those groups and others are being controlled by people who are seeking to continue and complete the 'Great Work of Ages' – the takeover of the planet and the human mind. How they propose to complete that task we will see later.

One of the most active Brotherhood organisations today are the Freemasons and they would seem to have their origins in Sumer and Egypt in the guilds of the stonemasons and craftsmen. These guilds copied many of the Brotherhood and mystery school traditions and initiations. The title Grand Master, which is common to most secret Brotherhood branches, was already being used at this time. Later, these guilds would evolve into freemasonry which is open to anyone considered acceptable (not just masons) and has been a front for some outrageous behaviour and manipulation. It aims, like the whole infiltrated Brotherhood through the centuries, to keep spiritual knowledge from the general population (the basis of that set out at the start of this book) and even twist the version it gives to its initiates. Freemasonry is, today, the major arm of the Brotherhood. Five thousand years after ancient Egypt, Albert Pike, a Grand Commander of the Supreme Council of Freemasonry in America, would describe this secret society as:

"The Custodian and depository of the great philosophical and religious truths unknown to the world at large, and handed down from age to age by an unbroken current of tradition, embodied in symbols, emblems, and allegories."

It is often asked who are 'they', the elite that researchers speak of in relation to the conspiracy to control the human race. How can such an ambition possibly have spanned thousands of years? As Pike said, the knowledge and the agenda are handed down through the generations. 'They' are people who have been accepted into the highest levels of initiation by the infiltrated Brotherhood societies. At any point in history over the last 5,000 years those accepted into the highest degrees have continued the Great Work, while looking for those with the potential to take over from them. So while the personnel change, the agenda and methods have remained very much the same. Only those considered certain to continue the work and keep it secret are accepted in the elite levels. One way potential "adepts" have been tested is by telling them to spit on the cross. Those who refuse are congratulated for their commitment to serve God and reject such heresy. But they are never subsequently considered for promotion, because they cannot be trusted with the knowledge of the real agenda. Those who do spit on the cross are the ones who go on up the ladder because, among other things, they do as they are told.

It is part of the Freemasons' mythology that human civilisations were begun by visitors from the star Sirius which they connect with the Egyptian goddess, Isis. Sumerian stories record that these ETs were fish-like in their appearance – the 'Oannes' I mentioned before – and that they passed on information about building, spiritual symbolism, science and arts. The Egyptians certainly acknowledged the importance of Sirius to them. The Freemasonic and Brotherhood symbol of the pyramid with the capstone depicted as the all-seeing eye goes back to these ancient times. This is said to represent the eye of Sirius – although I see it as Lucifer. The

Dogon people in Mali, in sub-Saharan Africa, have had a legend, probably originating in Egypt, which has been passed on over five thousand years. It tells of a star that they claimed orbited Sirius. They knew it as the smallest and heaviest of stars containing the germs of all things and the Dogons said that it weighed so much that 'all the Earthly beings combined cannot lift it'. The legend further claims that it took fifty years for the star to orbit Sirius.

All this is remarkable when you think that the star they have known about for thousands of years was not officially discovered until the last century and was photographed for the first time in 1970. It has been named Sirius B, and the Dogons have been proved correct in their claims. For it does take around fifty years to complete an orbit and scientists have suggested that one cubic foot of Sirius B matter would weigh 2,000 tons. Obviously, Sirius is of considerable relevance to what has been happening on this planet. How could Earth people know such details unless they were told by those who knew? Extra-terrestrials or highly accurate channelling.

Freemasonry, like most secret societies of the infiltrated Brotherhood, bases its beliefs and aims on the worship of the Sun God and Mother Goddess mythology which it is believed was common to ancient civilisations. This Father/Mother belief was reflected in the Egyptian trinity of gods – Osiris, the father, Isis, the mother, and Horus, the son. Another name often used for the Brotherhood is its Latin name, the Illuminati, or 'illuminated ones'. It may sound fantastic at this stage in our story, but the world is controlled today by a Brotherhood of secret societies which go back to this period. The swastika, the lamb, the obelisk, the apron, which some Egyptian gods are depicted as wearing, and, of course, the pyramid and eye are still the symbols of the Brotherhood societies. Thousands of years after ancient Egypt you can find the pyramid and eye symbol very easily in America. It forms the reverse of the Great Seal of the United States and appears on every dollar bill. The truths pedalled by the negative secret societies have been twisted enough to mislead their members. I feel the Egyptian beliefs have been misrespresented to an extent, but, as one researcher said so correctly, it doesn't matter if what they believe is true or even if *you* believe it. As long as *they* believe it, we are all affected by the way their thinking influences their actions.

Channelling was at the centre of the Egyptian culture and could be used to control or, as it was in many cases, to gather knowledge that was not being made available from elsewhere. Just as the Luciferic consciousness wishes to control people, so the consciousness of 'The Light' wishes to set them free by allowing them access to the spiritual truths that are being denied them. Channelling is an important way of doing this. This is one reason why, despite the efforts of the manipulators, many people in Babylon and Egypt had more spiritual knowledge than the elite wanted them to know. Channellers were widely consulted as a source of divine inspiration and there were rooms called the holy of holies or sanctuaries where inter-frequency communications took place. These were built on energy points where a 'god' (a discarnate consciousness in this case) could communicate most effectively. This is how the prophets in the Bible got their information. Those in the Christian Church who equate channelling with devil worship should know that the term prophet comes from the Greek word which means medium!

In the early Egyptian period, some worshipped the Sun god *Ra*, and others followed the god Amun or Amen. These two later became fused into one, Amun or Amen Ra. After their prayers and religious teachings they would say the name of their god. This was passed on through Judaism into Christianity and, in churches all over the world today, Christians still end their prayers and readings with the word 'Amen'. How many know that, in doing so, they are saying the name of a Pagan god of channelled or extra-terrestrial origin, just as the Egyptians did? Amen also represents a sound, by the way, that resonates a certain frequency known to the ancients. Egyptian mythology had a trinity of gods in Osiris, the father, Isis, the mother, and Horus, the son. The Egyptians believed that Osiris came to suffer so that those who believed in him would live. He was known as Lord of Eternity, the Judge and Saviour of the human race, the Resurrection and the Life, the Bread of Life, the Redeemer and Mediator who would decide the eternal fate of heaven or hell for the dead. Horus was portrayed sitting on his mother's knee and, from this, the idea of the Madonna and child was to emerge in Christianity. The Egyptian figure of evil, Set, became the Christian version, Satan. The cross was an Egyptian symbol for thousands of years before it was adopted by Christianity and the Egyptians celebrated the festival of Easter, the day that Horus, the son, was said to have died and risen again to become one with his father. All this would have been influenced by the Babylonian belief in Bel and both would have begun with the same channelled communications or extra-terrestrial influence. In fact, I think that most of this symbolism relates back to extra-terrestrial activities and the star systems they came from, and from the knowledge that the day was approaching when the forces of disharmony (Set, Satan, Lucifer etc) would be overcome by harmony. That time is now.

The idea of a trinity of gods, or three gods in one, is a theme that runs through countless pre-Christian religions. The Christians merely copied it as they copied everything else. Some of the symbolism of the trinity is linked to energy balancing. The three points of the triangle stand for positive/negative/balance, and male/female/balance. The triangle is a well-known esoteric symbol as is the double interconnecting triangle known as the Star of David. This represents the balance of the spiritual with the balance of the physical.

Thousands of years before Christianity, dogmatic religious belief, based on the misunderstandings and twisted truths I have highlighted, was already being used by the Luciferic consciousness in its many guises to close down the potential of the human mind and to fill it with myths and the literal interpretation of symbolic stories. The fear of the gods and the horrors that would be visited upon those who did not do as they were told was a very effective way of keeping the masses from the knowledge of their true selves. The god kings of the various cultures and the gathering power of the priests as interpreters of the gods' desires added to the expansion of the religious dogma and control.

The Egyptian elite were an advanced people for their time in many ways, although they kept most of the population in physical and spiritual slavery. They performed operations – mummies have been found with well-set fractures and false teeth. It was to be many thousands of years before anything like this appeared in Europe. Educated Egyptians understood the principles of astronomy and astrology, as did the Babylonians. Astronomy and astrology were seen as indivisible sciences. The richer Egyptians lived in beautiful homes with elegant furniture and artwork. In England, three thousand years later, some Christian clergy were still condemning the use of knives and forks as the work of the devil.

The culture and belief systems developed in Mesopotamia and Egypt, possibly under the influence of extra-terrestrials and channelled sources, were to have a fundamental impact on all that followed. India was also developing a distinct culture in the pre-

Christian world but, again, the basis of the Hindu religion was
inherited from the West when Aryan peoples invaded around
1500BC and turned the Indians into their servants. The gods of
India, therefore, have a somewhat familiar ring. The father god of
the Hindus is Brahma and he is part of a trinity of gods which
includes Krishna, their version of the Jesus-type figure. Krishna is
the Hindu saviour (see Bel, Osiris, etc). He is said to have lived
around 1,000BC and is still revered today in much the same way as
Jesus. The texts from which Hinduism was created are called the
Vedas and in them you can find references which appear to record
extra- terrestrial activities. Hinduism was a religion introduced by
the invaders to create a strict system of hierarchy known as castes.
It was a means to divide and rule. The religious apartheid which
Hinduism promotes with its castes, taboos and impositions is a
continuing confirmation, as with most religion, that large areas of
incarnate humanity are yet to evolve from spiritual childhood.
But, if you want a system of control, it's wonderful and it is being
used in that way today just as it was by the Aryans. Missionaries
from the Egyptian Brotherhood also arrived in India during and
after the invasion and, as a consequence, its power began to expand
rapidly. India is, today, a major centre of Brotherhood activity.

Five hundred years after the physical life claimed for Krishna
came Gautama Buddha which translates as Guatama the Enlightened. Today he is known simply as Buddha and, in his name,
the religion of Buddhism has flourished. Buddha was born in India
into a royal family. He was a prince, but he gave up this privilege
and wealth to spread his philosophy which incorporated reincarna-
tion and an ethical way of life based on peace and love. I don't
agree with all that he believed in but there is much that I can easily
support. He spoke out against the priests of the day and encouraged the pursuit of truth, wisdom and knowledge. He talked of a
universal brotherhood (the positive variety!) and equal rights for
men and women. Buddha spoke simple truths. He had no desire to
be turned into some saviour-god or to be worshipped by followers
who complicated his simple philosophy with additions, ceremonies and hierarchies. All he stood for – and all we ever really
need – are spiritual knowledge, not endless 'isms' to complicate
them.

After Buddha's physical release, his beliefs became the dominant
religion in India. In the third century, King Asoka would adopt
Buddhism and send his representatives across the known world to